Withdrawn

Praise for
SIX DEGREES of SEPARATION

"Guare transports the audience...to the magical reaches of the imagination...Cyclonic action, ranging from knock-about farce to hallucinatory dreams....Among the many remarkable aspects of Mr. Guare's writing is the seamlessness of his imagery, characters and themes, as if this play had just erupted from his imagination in one perfect piece. ...As conversant with Cezanne and the Sistine Chapel as it is with Sotheby's and 'Starlight Express,' this work aspires to the classical esthetics and commensurate unity that are missing in the...fragmented 20th-century lives it illuminates. That spirit shines through....A transcendent theatrical experience that is itself a lasting vision of the humane new world of which Mr. Guare and his New Yorkers so hungrily dream."

—*The New York Times*

"A fast, dense, wildly imaginative tragicomedy that... manages to be both merciless and compassionate about rich people, ghetto opportunists, unhappy families, the mega-art world, Holden Caulfield, South African whites, the star-struck, the homeless, the liberal chic, and the manipulative of many persuasions....How good to have Guare's voice back."

—*Newsday*

Also by John Guare

PLAYS

Muzeeka
Cop-Out
House of Blue Leaves
Rich and Famous
Marco Polo Sings a Solo
Landscape of the Body
Bosoms and Neglect
Lydie Breeze
Gardenia
Women and Water

MUSICALS

Two Gentlemen of Verona
(after Shakespeare: with Mel Shapiro and Galt MacDermot)
The Race to Urga
(from Brecht's *The Exception*; Lincoln Center Theater Workshop:
with Leonard Bernstein, Jerome Robbins and
Stephen Sondheim)

SCREENPLAYS

Taking Off
(collaboration with Milos Forman and
Jean-Claude Carrière)

Atlantic City

Six Degrees *of* Separation

Six Degrees of Separation

a play by

John Guare

RANDOM HOUSE · NEW YORK

Six Degrees of Separation began performances on 19 May 1990 at the Mitzi E. Newhouse Theater, Lincoln Center Theater, Gregory Mosher, Director, Bernard Gersten, Executive Producer.

The cast was as follows:

OUISA	Stockard Channing
FLAN	John Cunningham
GEOFFREY	Sam Stoneburner
PAUL	James McDaniel
HUSTLER	David Eigenberg
KITTY	Kelly Bishop
LARKIN	Peter Maloney
DETECTIVE	Brian Evers
TESS	Robin Morse
WOODY	Gus Rogerson
BEN	Anthony Rapp
DR. FINE	Stephen Pearlman
DOUG	Evan Handler
POLICEMAN/DOORMAN	Philip LeStrange
TRENT	John Cameron Mitchell
RICK	Paul McCrane
ELIZABETH	Mari Nelson

Tony Walton designed the sets, William Ivey Long the costumes, and Paul Gallo the lights.

The director was Jerry Zaks.

Between August 1 and October 28, Kelly Bishop and then Swoosie Kurtz played Ouisa. Gregory Simmons and then Courtney B. Vance played Paul.

On 8 November 1990, the production moved to the Vivian Beaumont Theater, Lincoln Center, with Courtney B. Vance playing Paul, Robert Duncan McNeill playing Rick, and Stockard Channing returning to the role of Ouisa.

Armed with a lot of preparation, I wrote *Six Degrees of Separation* very quickly. (The question actors get asked is: How do you remember the lines? The question playwrights get is: How long did it take you to write it? The answer on this one from a playwright born in 1938 about a play written in 1989 is fifty-one years.) I brought *Six Degrees* to Lincoln Center Theater, which had produced the 1986 revival of *House of Blue Leaves*. Gregory Mosher and Bernard Gersten, the director and executive producer of Lincon Center Theater, read it and put the play into immediate production, making it a rarity in today's theater: no workshop, no readings, and seventeen actors. Lincoln Center reassembled most of the *Blue Leaves* design staff. Jerry Zaks, who'd directed *Blue Leaves*, agreed to direct. We began auditions in October and saw an average of fifty actors for thirteen of the roles. We used that time of casting to discuss the play, to understand the rhythm of the play, to hear what the play wanted to be. All I knew about the play was that it had to go like the wind.

Jerry Zaks felt it crucial to translate that speed into stage terms. The play was to open at the Mitzi E. Newhouse Theater, which has a thrust stage, meaning the audience sits three-quarters of the way around the stage. Meaning it's ideal for a play that addresses the audience in a very intimate, friendly fashion. Meaning also it's a long way for entrances and exits and pulse-killing scene changes. Jerry met the challenge. He and Tony Walton devised a production scheme whereby the actors (except Paul, the Hustler, and the Doorman) sit in the front row for the course of the performance, appearing and vanishing, handing up, holding up, and receiving props and costumes as needed.

We decided that when anyone speaks on the phone, he or she simply steps into a special light that lasts for the length of the conversation. No one mimes handling a phone. They just talk. A click signifies the call's termination.

Tony Walton designed a deceptively simple set: a bright red carpeted disc, two red sofas, and, hanging over the stage, a framed double-sided Kandinsky which slowly revolved before the play began and when it was over. He encased the back wall, made of black scrim, in a gilt picture frame and then divided that into two levels. The openings on either level were framed in gold. When actors appeared in the upper level doors, the set would give the feeling that they floated in the dark. The geometric interplay between the circle of the bright red disc and the rectangle of the back wall caused a palpable tension.

The audience only sees through the black scrim once: when Ouisa goes down the hall and opens the door.

Paul Gallo's lights defined the different locations and changes of time. William Ivey Long costumed the actors in vivid stained-glass colors.

Rehearsals began. Oh boy. We had made one casting error, which rectified itself after two days but left us stranded with sixteen actors and no lead. Every actress we wanted was working. Or busy. Or out of town. We kept rehearsing. We went into our second week of rehearsal with no lead. Peter Maloney's wife, Kristin Griffith, filled in. Steven Beckler, the stage manager, filled in. One morning we read in the paper that a play, starring Stockard Channing, expected to open next on Broadway would instead terminate its run in San Diego. Stockard had been nominated for a Tony for her work in *House of Blue Leaves*. We sent her the script. Stockard, the exemplar trouper, closed in San Diego on a Sunday and came to us on Tuesday and we didn't miss a beat. Has any other actress been scheduled to open in New York at a certain time and indeed did open at that time, however in another play?

Our original ten-week run was extended. Magazines did stories on people hopefully waiting in line for ticket cancellations. Stockard left temporarily to honor a movie commitment made when we were on a limited run. Swoosie Kurtz, who'd won the Tony for *Blue Leaves* and had been shooting a pilot during our rehearsal panic, came in and was brilliant for nine weeks. James McDaniel left to go into a TV series. Courtney B. Vance succeeded happily into the part and would remain with it when Swoosie left at the end of October to do her TV series and Stockard would return for a now-indefinite run upstairs at the Vivian Beaumont Theater.

The experience has been remarkably happy. I wrote this play for a specific theater and they did it. It's a wonderful thing for a playwright in the 1990s to belong to a theater.

What else to say?

Six Degrees of Separation is performed without an intermission and takes approximately ninety minutes to perform.

SIX DEGREES *of* SEPARATION

A painting revolves slowly high over the stage. The painting is by Kandinsky. He has painted on either side of the canvas in two different styles. One side is geometric and somber. The other side is wild and vivid. The painting stops its revolve and opts for the geometric side.

A couple runs on stage, in nightdress, very agitated. FLANDERS KITTREDGE *is 44.* LOUISA KITTREDGE *is 43. They are very attractive. They speak to us.*

OUISA

Tell them!

FLAN

I am shaking.

OUISA

You have to do *something*!

FLAN

It's awful.

OUISA

Is anything gone?

FLAN

How can I look? I'm shaking.

OUISA *(To us)*

Did he take anything?

FLAN

Would you concentrate on yourself?

OUISA

I want to know if anything's gone?

FLAN *(To us)*

We came in the room.

OUISA

I went in first. You didn't see what I saw.

FLAN

Calm down.

OUISA

We could have been killed.

FLAN

The silver Victorian inkwell.

OUISA

How can you think of *things*? We could have been murdered.

*(An actor appears for a moment holding up an ornate Victorian
inkwell capped by a silver beaver.)*

FLAN

There's the inkwell. Silver beaver. Why?

OUISA

Slashed—our throats slashed.

(Another actor appears for a moment holding up a framed portrait of a dog, say, a pug.)

FLAN

And there's the watercolor. Our dog.

OUISA

Go to bed at night happy and then murdered. Would we have woken up?

FLAN

Now I lay me down to sleep—the most terrifying words—just think of it—

OUISA

I pray the Lord my soul to keep—

FLAN

The nightmare part—If I should die before I wake—

OUISA

If I should die—I pray the Lord my soul to take—

FLAN AND OUISA

Oh.

OUISA

It's awful.

FLAN

We're alive.

(FLAN stops, frightened suddenly, listening.)

FLAN

Hello?

(He holds her.)

FLAN

Hello!

OUISA *(Whispers)*

You don't call out Hello unless—

FLAN

I think we'd tell if someone else were here.

OUISA

We didn't all night. Oh, it was awful awful awful awful.

(They pull off their robes and are smartly dressed for dinner.)

FLAN *(To us)*

We were having a wonderful evening last night.

OUISA *(To us)*

A friend we hadn't seen for many years came by for dinner.

FLAN *(Portentously)*

A friend from South Africa—

OUISA

Don't say it so portentously.

FLAN *(Bright)*

A friend from South Africa.

OUISA

Don't be ga-ga.

FLAN *(To us)*

I'm an art dealer. Private sales. Purchases.

OUISA *(To us)*

We knew our friend from South Africa

FLAN

through our children when they all lived in New York.

OUISA

They had gone back to South Africa.

FLAN

He was here in New York briefly on business and asked us to ask him for dinner.

OUISA

He's King Midas rich. Literally. Gold mines.

FLAN

Seventy thousand workers in just one gold mine.

OUISA

But he is always short of cash because his government won't let its people—

FLAN

its white people—

OUISA

—its white people take out any money. So it's like taking in a War Baby.

FLAN

When he called it was like a bolt from the blue as I had
a deal coming up and was short by

OUISA

two million.

FLAN

The figure is superfluous.

OUISA

I hate when you use the word "superfluous." I mean,
he needed two million and we hadn't seen Geoffrey
in a long time and while Geoffrey might not have
the price of a dinner he easily might have two million
dollars.

FLAN

The currents last night were very churny.

OUISA

We weren't sucking up. We like Geoffrey.

FLAN

It's that awful thing of having truly rich folk for
friends.

OUISA

Face it. The money does get in the—

FLAN

Only if you let it. The fact of the money shouldn't get
in—

OUISA

Having a rich friend is like drowning and your friend

makes life boats. But the friend gets very touchy if you say one word: life boat. Well, that's two words. We were afraid our South African friend might say "You only love me for my life boats?" But we *like* Geoffrey.

FLAN
It wasn't a life-threatening evening.

OUISA
Rich people can do something for you even if you're not sure what it is you want them to do.

FLAN
Hardly a life boat evening—

OUISA (*Sing-song*)
Portentous.

FLAN
But when he called and asked us to take him for dinner, he made a sudden pattern in life's little tea leaves because who wants to go to banks? Geoffrey called and our tempests settled into showers and life was manageable. What more can you want?

(**GEOFFREY** *is there, an elegant, impeccably British South African, slightly older than* OUISA *and* FLAN. FLAN *passes drinks.*)

GEOFFREY
Listen. (*They do.*)
It always amazes me when New York is so quiet.

OUISA
With the kids away, we get used to a lower noise quotient.

FLAN
Geoffrey, you have to move out of South Africa. You'll
be killed. Why do you stay in South Africa?

GEOFFREY
One has to stay there to educate the black workers and
we'll know we've been successful when they kill us.

FLAN
Planning the revolution that will destroy you.

OUISA
Putting your life on the line.

GEOFFREY
You don't think of it like that. I wish you'd come visit.

OUISA
But we'd visit you and sit in your gorgeous house
planning trips into the townships demanding to see
the poorest of the poor. "Are you sure they're the
worst off? I mean, we've come all this way. We don't
want to see people just mildly victimized by apart-
heid. We demand shock." It doesn't seem right sitting
on the East Side talking about revolution.

FLAN
Only small murky cafes for Pepe le Moko here.

OUISA
No. La Pasionaria. I will come to South Africa and
build barricades and lean against them, singing.

FLAN
And the people would follow.

OUISA

"Follow Follow Follow." What's that song?

FLAN

The way Gorbachev cheered on the striking coal miners in the Ukraine—yes, you must strike—it is your role in history to dismantle this system. Russia and Poland—you can't believe the developments in the world—*The Fantasticks*, "Follow Follow Follow."

OUISA

China.

FLAN and OUISA *(Despair)*

Oh.

GEOFFREY

Oy vay China. As my grandmother would say.
(They all laugh.)
Our role in history. And we offer ourselves up to it.

FLAN

That is your role in history. Not our role.

OUISA

A role in history. To say that so easily.

FLAN *(To* GEOFFREY*)*

Do you want another drink before we go out?

OUISA

The phrase—striking coal miners—I see all these very striking coal miners modelling the fall fashions—

GEOFFREY

Where should we?

FLAN

There's good Szechuan. And Hunan

OUISA

The sign painter screwed up the sign. Instead of The Hunan Wok, he painted The Human Wok.

GEOFFREY

God! The restaurants! New York has become the Florence of the sixteenth century. Genius on every corner.

OUISA

I don't think genius has kissed the Human Wok.

GEOFFREY

The new Italian looked cheery.

FLAN and OUISA

Good.

FLAN

We made reservations.

OUISA

They wrap ravioli up like salt water taffy.

FLAN

Six on a plate for a few hundred dollars.

GEOFFREY

You have to come to South Africa so I can pay you back. I'll take you on my plane into the Okavango Swamps—

OUISA

Did you hear—to take back to Johannesburg. Out in East Hampton

FLAN

last weekend

OUISA

a guy goes into one of the better food stores—

FLAN

Dean and DeLuca—

OUISA

one of the Dean and DeLuca look alikes. Gets a pack of cigarettes and an ice cream bar. Goes up front. Sees there's a line at the register. Slaps down two twenty dollar bills and goes out.

FLAN

We sent it to the *Times*.

OUISA

They have the joke page of things around New York.

FLAN

They send you a bottle of champagne.

(They all laugh brightly.)

OUISA *(To us)*

We weren't auditioning but I kept thinking Two million dollars two million dollars.

FLAN *(To us)*

It's like when people say 'Don't think about elephants' and all you can think about is elephants elephants.

OUISA *(To us)*

Two million dollars two million dollars.

(They laugh brightly. The doorbell rings.)

OUISA *(To* FLAN*)*
Whatever you do, don't think about elephants.

*(*OUISA *goes.)*

GEOFFREY
Elephants?

FLAN
Louisa is a Dada manifesto.

GEOFFREY
Tell me about the Cezanne?

FLAN
Mid-period. Landscape of a dark green forest. In the far distance you see the sunlight. One of his first uses of a pale color being forced to carry the weight of the picture. The experiment that would pay off in the apples. A burst of color asked to carry so much. The Japanese don't like anything about it except it's a Cezanne—

*(A young black man—*PAUL*—enters, supported by* THE DOOR-MAN. PAUL *is in his early twenties, very handsome, very preppy. He has been beaten badly. Blood seeps through his white Brooks Brothers shirt.*
OUISA *follows at a loss.*
THE DOORMAN *helps* PAUL *to the sofa and stands at the door warily.)*

PAUL
I'm so sorry to bother you, but I've been hurt and I've

lost everything and I didn't know where to go. Your
children—I'm a friend of—

OUISA *(To us)*

And he mentioned our daughter's name.

FLAN *(To us)*

And the school where they went.

OUISA *(To FLAN)*

Harvard. You can say Harvard.

FLAN *(To us)*

We don't want to get into libel.

PAUL

I was mugged. Out there. In Central Park. By the
statue of that Alaskan husky. I was standing there trying to figure out why there is a statue of a dog who
saved lives in the Yukon in Central Park and I was
standing there trying to puzzle it out when—

OUISA

Are you okay?

PAUL

They took my money and my briefcase. I said my
thesis is in there—

FLAN

His shirt's bleeding.

OUISA

His shirt is not bleeding. *He's* bleeding.

PAUL *(A wave of nausea)*
I get this way around blood.

FLAN
Not on the rug.

PAUL
I don't mind the money. But in this age of mechanical reproduction they managed to get the only copy of my thesis.

FLAN
Eddie, get the doctor—

PAUL
No! I'll survive.

FLAN
You'll be fine.

(FLAN *helps* PAUL *out of the room.* THE DOORMAN *goes.*)

OUISA *(To us)*
We bathed him. We did First Aid.

GEOFFREY *(Leaving)*
It's been wonderful seeing you—

OUISA *(Very cheery)*
No no no! Stay!—
(To us) Two million dollars two million dollars—

GEOFFREY
My time is so short—before I leave America, I really should see—

FLAN *(Calling from the hall)*
Where are the bandages!?—

OUISA
The Red Cross advises: Press edges of the wound
firmly together, wash area with water—

GEOFFREY
May I use your phone?

OUISA
You darling old poop—just sit back—this'll only take
a mo—
(Calling) Flan, go into Woody's room and get him a
clean shirt.
Geoffrey, have you seen the new book on Cezanne?
(To us) I ran down the hall to get the book on Cezanne,
got the gauze from my bathroom, gave the Cezanne to
Flan who wanted the gauze, gave the gauze to Geoffrey who wanted Cezanne. Two million dollars two
million dollars—

(FLAN comes back in the room.)

FLAN
He's going to be fine.

OUISA *(To us)*
And peace was restored.

*(PAUL enters, slightly recovered, wearing a clean pink shirt. He
winces as he pulls on his blazer.)*

PAUL
Your children said you were kind. All the kids were

sitting around the dorm one night dishing the shit out
of their parents. But your kids were silent and said,
No, not our parents. Not Flan and Ouisa. Not the Kittredges. The Kittredges are kind. So after the muggers
left, I looked up and saw these Fifth Avenue apart-
ments. Mrs. Onassis lives there. I know the Babcocks
live over there. The Auchinclosses live there. But you
lived here. I came here.

OUISA

Can you believe what the kids said?

FLAN *(To us)*

We mentioned our kids names.

OUISA

We can mention our kids' names. Our children are not
going to sue us for using their names.

PAUL

But your kids—I love them. Talbot and Woody mean
the world to me.

FLAN

He lets you call him Woody? Nobody's called him
Woody in years.

PAUL

They described this apartment in detail. The Kandinsky!—that's a double. One painted on either side.

FLAN

We flip it around for variety.

PAUL

It's wonderful.

FLAN *(To us)*

Wassily Kandinsky. Born 1866 Moscow. Blue Rider Exhibition 1914. He said "It is clear that the choice of object that is one of the elements in the harmony of form must be decided only by a corresponding vibration in the human soul." Died 1944 France.

PAUL

It's the way they said it would be.

OUISA *(To us)*

Geoffrey had been silent up to now.

GEOFFREY

Did you bitch your parents?

PAUL

As a matter of fact. No. Your kids and I...we both liked our parents...loved our—look, am I getting in the way? I burst in here, hysterical. Blood. I didn't mean to—

FLAN and OUISA

No!

OUISA

Tell us about our children.

FLAN *(To us)*

Three. Two at Harvard. Another girl at Groton.

OUISA

How is Harvard?

PAUL

Well, fine. It's just there. Everyone's in a constant state

of luxurious despair and constant discovery and
paralysis.

OUISA *(To us)*
We asked him where home was.

FLAN *(To us)*
Out West, he said.

PAUL
Although I've lived all over. My folks are divorced.
He's remarried. He's doing a movie.

OUISA
He's in the movies?

PAUL
He's directing this one but he does act.

FLAN
What's he directing?

PAUL
Cats.

OUISA
Someone is directing a film of *Cats?*

FLAN
Don't be snooty.

PAUL
You've seen it? T.S. Eliot—

FLAN
Well, yes. Years ago.

OUISA

A benefit for some disease or school—

FLAN

Surely they can't make the movie of *Cats*.

OUISA

Of course they can.

PAUL

They're going to try. My father'll be here auditioning—

OUISA

Cats?

PAUL

He's going to use people.

OUISA

What a courageous stand!

PAUL

They thought of lots of ways to go. Animation.

FLAN

Animation would be nice.

PAUL

But he found a better way. As a matter of fact, he turned it down at first. He went to tell the producers— as a courtesy—all the reasons why you couldn't make a movie of *Cats* and in going through all the reasons why you couldn't make a movie of *Cats*, he suddenly saw how you could make a movie of *Cats*—

OUISA

Eureka in the bathtub. How wonderful.

FLAN

May we ask who—

OUISA *(To us)*

And it was here we pulled up—ever so slightly—pulled up closer—

FLAN *(To us)*

And he told us.

OUISA *(To us)*

He named the greatest black star in movies. Sidney—

FLAN

Don't say it. We're trying to keep this abstract. Plus libel laws.

OUISA

Sidney Poitier! There. I don't care. We have to have truth. *(To us)* He started out as a lawyer and is terrified of libel. I'm not.

(PAUL *steps forward cheerily.*)

PAUL *(To us)*

Sidney Poitier, the future Jackie Robinson of films, was born the twenty-fourth of February 1927 in Miami during a visit his parents made to Florida—legally?—to sell tomatoes they had grown on their farm in the Bahamas. He grew up on Cat Island, "so poor they didn't even own dirt" he has said. Neglected by his family, my father would sit on the shore, and, as he told me many times, "conjure up the kind of worlds

that were on the other side and what I'd do in them."
He arrived in New York City from the Bahamas in the
winter of 1943 at age fifteen and a half and lived in the
pay toilet of the bus station across from the old Madi-
son Square Garden at Fiftieth and Eighth Avenue. He
moved to the roof of the Brill Building, commonly
known as Tin Pan Alley, and washed dishes at the Turf
Restaurant for $4.11 a night. He taught himself to read
by reading the newspaper. In the black newspaper,
the theater page was opposite the want ad page.
Among his 42 films are *No Way Out*, 1950; *Cry the
Beloved Country*, 1952; *Blackboard Jungle*, 1955; *The Defi-
ant Ones*, 1958; *Raisin in the Sun*, 1961; *Lilies of the Field*,
1963; *In the Heat of the Night*, 1967; *To Sir With Love*,
1967; *Shoot to Kill*, 1988; and, of course, *Guess Who's
Coming to Dinner*. He won the Oscar for *Lilies of the Field*
and was twice named top male box-office star in the
country. My father made no films from 1977 to 1987
but worked as director and author. Dad said to me
once, "I still don't fully understand how all that came
about in the sequence it came about."

(PAUL *returns to the sofa.*)

PAUL

Dad's not in till tomorrow at the Sherry. I came down
from Cambridge. Thought I'd stay at some fleabag for
adventure. Orwell. Down and Out. I really don't know
New York. I know Rome and Paris and Los Angeles a
lot better.

OUISA

We're going out to dinner. You'll come.

PAUL

Out to dinner?

FLAN

Out to dinner.

PAUL

But why go out to dinner?

OUISA

Because we have reservations and oh my god what time is it? Have we lost the reservations and we don't have a damn thing in the house and it's sixteenth-century Florence and there's genius on every block.

GEOFFREY

Don't mock.

(She kisses GEOFFREY.)

PAUL

You must have something in the fridge.

FLAN

A frozen steak from the Ice Age.

PAUL

Why spend a hundred dollars on a bowl of rice? Let me into the kitchen. Cooking calms me. What I'd like to do is calm down, pay back your kids—

OUISA *(To us)*

He mentioned our kids names—

FLAN *(To us)*

Two. Two at Harvard. A daughter at Groton.

PAUL

who've been wonderful to me.

OUISA

They've never mentioned you.

FLAN

What are they supposed to say? We've become friends with the son of Sidney Poitier, barrier breaker of the fifties and sixties?

GEOFFREY

Your father means a great deal in South Africa.

OUISA *(To us)*

Even Geoffrey was touched.

PAUL

I'm glad of that. Dad and I went to Russia once to a film festival and he was truly amazed how much his presence meant—

OUISA

Oh no! Tell us stories of movie stars tying up their children and being cruel.

PAUL

I wish.

GEOFFREY

You wish?

PAUL

If I wanted to write a book about him, I really couldn't. No one would want to read it. He's decent. I admire him.

OUISA

He's married to an actress who was in one of—she's white? Am I right?

PAUL

That is not my mother. That is his second wife. He met Joanna making *The Lost Man*. He left my mother, who had stuck by him in the lean years. I had just been born. *The Lost Man* is the only film of my father's I can't bring myself to see.

OUISA

Oh, I'm sorry. We didn't mean to—

PAUL *(Bright)*

No! We're all good friends now. His kids from that marriage. Us—the old kids. I'd love to get in that kitchen.

FLAN *(To* OUISA*)*

What should we do?

OUISA *(To us)*

It's Geoffrey's only night in New York.

GEOFFREY

I vote stay in.

OUISA, FLAN and PAUL

Good!

*(*PAUL *goes off to the kitchen.)*

OUISA *(To us)*

We moved into the kitchen.

FLAN *(To us)*

We watched him cook.

OUISA *(To us)*

We watched him cook and chop.

FLAN *(To us)*

He sort of did wizardry—

OUISA *(To us)*

An old jar of sun-dried tomatoes—

FLAN *(To us)*

Leftovers—tuna fish—olives—onions—

(PAUL returns with three dishes heaped with food.)

PAUL

Here's dinner. All ready.

OUISA

Shall we move into the dining room?

PAUL

No, let's stay in here. It's nice in here.

(OUISA, FLAN and GEOFFREY take plates skeptically.)

OUISA

Have you declared your major yet?

PAUL

You're like all parents. What's your major?

FLAN

Geoffrey, Harvard has all those great titles the students give courses.

OUISA

The Holocaust and Ethics—

FLAN

Krauts and Doubts.

(They eat. Surprise. It's delicious.)

GEOFFREY

This is the best pasta I've ever—

PAUL

My father insisted we learn to cook.

FLAN

Isn't he from Jamaica? There's a taste of—

GEOFFREY

The islands.

PAUL

Yes. Before he made it, he ran four restaurants in Harlem. You have good buds!

GEOFFREY

See? Good buds. I've never been complimented on my buds—

PAUL *(To* GEOFFREY*)*

You're from—

GEOFFREY

Johannesburg.

(Pause)

PAUL

My dad took me to a movie shot in South Africa. The camera moved from this vile rioting in the streets to a villa where people picked at lunch on a terrace, the only riot the flowers and the birds—gorgeous plumage and petals. And I didn't understand. And Dad said to me, "You meet these young blacks who are having a terrible time. They've had a totally inadequate education and yet in '76—the year of the Soweto riots—they took on a tremendous political responsibility. It just makes you wonder at the maturity that is in them. It makes you realize that the 'crummy childhood' theory, that everything can be blamed in a Freudian fashion on the fact that you've had a bad upbringing, just doesn't hold water." Is everything okay?

(FLAN, OUISA and GEOFFREY are mesmerized, and then resume eating.)

FLAN, OUISA and GEOFFREY (While eating)
Mmmmmm...yes.

GEOFFREY
What about being black in America?

PAUL
My problem is I've never felt American. I grew up in Switzerland. Boarding school. Villa Rosey.

OUISA
There is a boarding school in Switzerland that takes you at age eighteen months.

PAUL
That's not me. I've never felt people liked me for my connections. Movie star kid problems. None of those. May I?

FLAN
Oh, please.

(PAUL pours a brandy.)

PAUL

But I never knew I was black in that racist way till I was sixteen and came back here. Very protected. White servants. After the divorce we moved to Switzerland, my mother, brother and I. I don't feel American. I don't even feel black. I suppose that's very lucky for me even though Freud says there's no such thing as luck. Just what you make.

OUISA

Does Freud say that? I think we're lucky having this dinner. Isn't this the finest time? A toast to you.

GEOFFREY

To *Cats!*

FLAN

Blunt question. What's he like?

OUISA

Let's not be star fuckers.

FLAN

I'm not a star fucker.

PAUL

My father, being an actor, has no real identity. You say to him, Pop, what's new? And he says, "I got an interesting script today. I was asked to play a lumberjack up in the Yukon. Now, I've been trained as a preacher, but my church fell apart. My wife says we have to get money to get through this winter. And I sign up as part of this team where all my beliefs are challenged. But I hold firm. In spite of prejudice. Because I want to get back to you. Out of this forest, back to the church..." And my father is in tears and I say Pop, this is not a

real event, this is some script that was sent to you.
And my father says "I'm trying it out to see how it fits
on me." But he has no life—he has no memory—only
the scripts producers send him in the mail through his
agents. That's his past.

OUISA *(To us)*

I just loved the kid so much. I wanted to reach out to
him.

FLAN *(To us)*

And then we asked him what his thesis was on.

GEOFFREY

The one that was stolen. Please?

PAUL

Well...

A substitute teacher out on Long Island was dropped
from his job for fighting with a student. A few weeks
later, the teacher returned to the classroom, shot the
student unsuccessfully, held the class hostage and
then shot himself. Successfully. This fact caught my
eye: last sentence. *Times.* A neighbor described him as
a nice boy. Always reading *Catcher in the Rye.*

The nitwit—Chapman—who shot John Lennon said
he did it because he wanted to draw the attention of
the world to *The Catcher in the Rye* and the reading of
that book would be his defense.

And young Hinckley, the whiz kid who shot Reagan
and his press secretary, said if you want my defense all
you have to do is read *Catcher in the Rye.* It seemed to
be time to read it again.

FLAN

I haven't read it in years.

(OUISA *shushes* FLAN.)

PAUL

I borrowed a copy from a young friend of mine because I wanted to see what she had underlined and I read this book to find out why this touching, beautiful, sensitive story published in July 1951 had turned into this manifesto of hate.

I started reading. It's exactly as I remembered. Everybody's a phoney. Page two: "My brother's in Hollywood being a prostitute." Page three: "What a phony slob his father was." Page nine: "People never notice anything."

Then on page twenty-two my hair stood up. Remember Holden Caulfield—the definitive sensitive youth —wearing his red hunter's cap. "A deer hunter hat? Like hell it is. I sort of closed one eye like I was taking aim at it. This is a people-shooting hat. I shoot people in this hat."

Hmmm, I said. This book is preparing people for bigger moments in their lives than I ever dreamed of. Then on page eighty-nine: "I'd rather push a guy out the window or chop his head off with an ax than sock him in the jaw. I hate fist fights...what scares me most is the other guy's face..."

I finished the book. It's a touching story, comic because the boy wants to do so much and can't do anything. Hates all phoniness and only lies to others.

Wants everyone to like him, is only hateful, and is completely self-involved In other words, a pretty accurate picture of a male adolescent.

And what alarms me about the book—not the book so much as the aura about it—is this: The book is primarily about paralysis. The boy can't function. And at the end, before he can run away and start a new life, it starts to rain and he folds.

Now there's nothing wrong in writing about emotional and intellectual paralysis. It may indeed, thanks to Chekhov and Samuel Beckett, be the great modern theme.

The extraordinary last lines of *Waiting For Godot*— "Let's go." "Yes, let's go." Stage directions: They do not move.

But the aura around this book of Salinger's—which perhaps should be read by everyone *but* young men—is this: It mirrors like a fun house mirror and amplifies like a distorted speaker one of the great tragedies of our times—the death of the imagination.

Because what else is paralysis?

The imagination has been so debased that imagination—being imaginative—rather than being the lynchpin of our existence now stands as a synonym for something outside ourselves like science fiction or some new use for tangerine slices on raw pork chops— what an imaginative summer recipe—and *Star Wars*! So imaginative! And *Star Trek*—so imaginative! And *Lord of the Rings*—all those dwarves—so *imaginative*—

[margin handwriting: Imagination is important to share as well]

The imagination has moved out of the realm of being our link, our most personal link, with our inner lives and the world outside that world—this world we share. What is schizophrenia but a horrifying state where what's in here doesn't match up with what's out there?

Why has imagination become a synonym for style?

[handwritten: Guare talking]

I believe that the imagination is the passport we create to take us into the real world.

I believe the imagination is another phrase for what is most uniquely *us*.

Jung says the greatest sin is to be unconscious.

Our boy Holden says "What scares me most is the other guy's face—it wouldn't be so bad if you could both be blindfolded—most of the time the faces we face are not the other guys' but our own faces. And it's the worst kind of yellowness to be so scared of yourself you put blindfolds on rather than deal with yourself…"

To face ourselves.

That's the hard thing.

The imagination.

That's God's gift to make the act of self-examination bearable.

(*Pause*)

OUISA

Well, indeed.

(*Pause*)

FLAN

I hope your muggers read every word.

OUISA

Darling.

GEOFFREY

I'm going to buy a copy of *Catcher in the Rye* at the airport and read it.

OUISA

Cover to cover.

PAUL

I'll test you. I should be going.

FLAN

Where will you stay?

OUISA

Not some flea bag.

PAUL

I get into the Sherry tomorrow morning. It's not so far off. I can walk around. I don't think they'll mug me twice in one evening.

OUISA

You'll stay here tonight.

PAUL

No! I have to be there at seven.

OUISA

We'll get you up.

PAUL

I have to be at the hotel at seven sharp or Dad will
have a fit.

OUISA

Up at six-fifteen, which is any moment now, and we
have that wedding in Roxbury—

FLAN

There's an alarm in that room.

PAUL

If it's any problem—

FLAN

It's only a problem if you leave.

PAUL

Six-fifteen? I'll tiptoe out.

FLAN

And we want to be in *Cats*.

OUISA

Flan!

PAUL

It's done.

GEOFFREY

I'll fly back. With my wife.

OUISA

Pushy. Both of you.

PAUL

He's not. Dad said I could be in charge of the extras.
You'd just be extras. That's all I can promise.

FLAN

In cat suits?

PAUL

No. You can be humans.

FLAN

That's very important. It has to be in our contracts. We
are humans.

GEOFFREY

We haven't got any business done tonight.

FLAN

Forget it. It was only an evening at home.

OUISA

Whatever you do, don't think about elephants.

PAUL

Did I intrude?

FLAN and OUISA

No!

PAUL

I'm sorry—oh Christ—

GEOFFREY (*To* FLAN)

There's all ways of doing business. Flanders, walk me
to the elevator.

OUISA

Love to Diana.
(To us) We embraced. And Flan and Geoffrey left—

(FLAN and GEOFFREY go.
Pause. PAUL and OUISA look at each other. Is it uncomfortable?
Then:)

PAUL

Let me clean up—

OUISA

No! Leave it for—

PAUL

Nobody comes in on Sunday.

OUISA

Yvonne will be in on Tuesday.

PAUL

You'll have every bug in Christendom—

(They both reach for the dishes.)

OUISA

Let me—

(PAUL takes the dishes.)

PAUL

No. You watch. It gives me a thrill to be looked at.

(Pause. PAUL goes off.)

OUISA *(To us, amazed)*

He washed up.

(FLAN returns, amazed.)

FLAN

He's in.

OUISA

He's in?

FLAN

He's in for two million.

OUISA

Two million!

FLAN

He says the Cezanne is a great investment. We should get it for six million and sell it to the Tokyo bunch for ten.

OUISA

Happy days! Oh god!

(PAUL returns.)

PAUL

Two million dollars?

OUISA

Figure it out. He doesn't have the price of a dinner but he can cough up two million dollars and the Japs will go ten! Break all those dishes! Two million! Go to ten! And we put up nothing?

FLAN

He sold that Hockney print I know he bought for a hundred bucks fifteen years ago for thirty-four thousand dollars. Sotheby took their cut, sure, but still—Two million! Wildest dreams. Paul, I should give you a commission.

PAUL

Your kids said you were an art dealer. But you don't have a gallery. I don't understand—

FLAN

People want to sell privately. Not go through a gallery.

OUISA

A divorce. Taxes. Publicity.

FLAN

People come to me looking for a certain school of painting.

OUISA

A modern. Impressionist. Renaissance.

FLAN

But don't want museums to know where it is.

OUISA

Japanese.

FLAN

I've got Japanese looking for a Cezanne. I have a syndicate that will buy the painting. There is a great second-level Cezanne coming up for sale in a very messy divorce.

OUISA

Wife doesn't want hubby to know she owns a
Cezanne.

FLAN

I needed an extra two million. Geoffrey called. Invited
him here for dinner.

OUISA

Tonight was a very nervous very casual very big thing.

PAUL

I couldn't tell—

OUISA

All the better.

PAUL

I'm glad I helped—

OUISA

You were wonderful!

PAUL

I'm so pleased I was wonderful. All this *and* a pink
shirt.

OUISA

Keep it. Look at the time.

PAUL

It's going to be time for me to get up.

FLAN

Then we'll say our good-nights now.

PAUL

Oh Christ. Regretfully. I'll tiptoe.

(FLAN *takes out his wallet.*)

FLAN

Take fifty dollars.

OUISA

Give him fifty dollars.

PAUL

Don't need it.

OUISA

Suppose your father's plane is late?

FLAN

A strike. Air controllers.

OUISA

Walking-around money. I wouldn't want my kids to be stuck in the street without a nickel.

FLAN

And you saved us a fortune. Do you know what our bill would've been at that little Eye-tie store front?

OUISA

And we picked up two million dollars. One billionth of a percent commission is—

FLAN

Fifty dollars.

(FLAN *hands him the money.* PAUL *hesitates, then takes it.*)

PAUL

But I'll get it back to you tomorrow. I want my father to meet you.

OUISA

We'd love to. Bring him up for dinner.

PAUL

Could I?

FLAN

You see how easy it is.

OUISA

Sure. If Paul does the cooking. *(They all laugh.)*

FLAN, OUISA and PAUL

Good night.

(FLAN points PAUL to his room.)

FLAN

Second door on the right.

(PAUL goes. FLAN and OUISA get ready for bed, pulling on their robes.)

FLAN

I want to get on my knees and thank God—money—

OUISA

Who said when artists dream they dream of money? I must be such an artist. Bravo. Bravo.

FLAN

I don't want to lose our life here. I don't want all the

debt to pile up and crush us.

OUISA

It won't. We're safe.

FLAN

For a while. We almost lost it. If I didn't get this money, Ouisa, I would've lost the Cezanne. It would've gone. I had nowhere to get it.

OUISA

Why don't you tell me how much these things mean? You wait till the last minute—

FLAN

I don't want to worry you.

OUISA

Not worry me? I'm your partner.

(They embrace.)

FLAN

There is a God.

OUISA

And his name is—

FLAN

Geoffrey?

OUISA

Sidney.

(FLAN goes. OUISA curls up on the sofa.)

OUISA *(To us)*

I dreamt of Sidney Poitier and his rise to acclaim. I dreamt that Sidney Poitier sat at the edge of my bed and I asked him what troubled him. Sidney? What troubles you? Is it right to make a movie of *Cats*?

(PAUL appears as SIDNEY POITIER in dinner clothes.)

PAUL/SIDNEY

I'll tell you why I have to make a movie of *Cats*. I know what *Cats* is, Louisa. May I call you Louisa? I have no illusions about the merits of *Cats*. But the world has been too heavy with all the right-to-lifers. Protect the lives of the unborn. Constitutional amendments. Marches! When does life begin? Or the converse. The end of life. The right to die. Why is life at this point in the twentieth century so focused on the very beginning of life and the very end of life? What about the eighty years we have to live between those two inexorable bookends?

OUISA

And you can get all that into *Cats*?

PAUL/SIDNEY

I'm going to try.

OUISA

Thank you. Thank you. You shall.

(Darkness. Then FLAN appears.)

FLAN *(To us)*

This is what I dreamt. I didn't dream so much as realize this. I felt so close to the paintings. I wasn't just selling them like pieces of meat. I remembered why I loved paintings in the first place—what had got me into this—and I thought—dreamed—remembered—how easy it is for a painter to *lose* a painting. He can paint and paint—work on a canvas for months and one day he loses it—just loses the structure—loses the sense of it—you lose the painting.

When the kids were little, we went to a parents' meeting at their school and I asked the teacher why all her students were geniuses in the second grade? Look at the first grade. Blotches of green and black. Look at the third grade. Camouflage. But the second grade—your grade. Matisses everyone. You've made my child a Matisse. Let me study with you. Let me into second grade! What is your secret? And this is what she said: "Secret? I don't have any secret. I just know when to take their drawings away from them."

I dreamt of color. I dreamt of our son's pink shirt. I dreamt of pinks and yellows and the new van Gogh that MOMA got and the "Irises" that sold for 53.9 million and, wishing a van Gogh was mine, I looked at my English hand-lasted shoes and thought of van Gogh's tragic shoes. I remembered me as I was. A painter losing a painting. But a South African awaiting revolution came to dinner. We were safe.

(Darkness. OUISA *appears.)*

OUISA *(To us)*
And it was six AM and I woke up so happy looking at my clean kitchen, all the more memorable because the previous evening had left no traces, and the paper was at the front door and I sat in the kitchen happily doing

the crossword puzzle in ink. Everybody does it in ink. I never met one person who didn't say they did it in ink. And I'm doing the puzzle and I see the time and it's nearly seven and Paul had to meet his father and I didn't want him to be late and was he healthy after his stabbing?

I went down the hall to the room where we had put him. The hall is eighteen feet long. I stopped in front of the door. Paul? (*She calls into the darkness.*)

                    PAUL'S VOICE (*Moaning*)
Yes Yes

                         OUISA
Paul??

                    PAUL'S VOICE (*Moaning*)
Yes Yes

                         OUISA
Are you all right?

                    OUISA (*To us*)
I opened the door and turned on the light.

                    OUISA (*Screams*)
Flan!!!

(*The stage is blindingly bright.*
PAUL, *startled, sits up in bed.*
A naked guy stands up on the bed.)

                    HUSTLER
What the fuck is going on here? Who the fuck are you?!

OUISA

Flan!

FLAN

What is it?

(FLAN *appears from the dark, tying his robe around him.*
THE HUSTLER, *naked but for white socks, comes into the room.*)

HUSTLER

Hey! How ya doin'?

FLAN

Oh my God!

OUISA *(A scream)*

Ahhh!

(THE HUSTLER *stretches out on the sofa.*)

HUSTLER

I gotta get some sleep—

(PAUL *runs into the room pulling on his clothes.*)

PAUL

I can explain.

(PAUL *tosses* THE HUSTLER'S *clothes onto the sofa.*)

OUISA

You went out after we went to sleep and picked up this
thing?

PAUL

I am so sorry.

FLAN

You brought this thing into our house! Thing! Thing!
Get out! Get out of my house!

(FLAN *tips the sofa, hurling* THE HUSTLER *onto the floor.* THE
HUSTLER *leaps at* FLAN *threateningly.*)

OUISA

Stop it! He might have a gun!

HUSTLER

I might have a gun. I might have a knife.

OUISA

He has a gun! He has a knife!

(THE HUSTLER *chases* OUISA *around the room.*)

PAUL

I can explain!

FLAN

Give me my fifty dollars.

PAUL

I spent it.

OUISA

Get out!

FLAN

Take your clothes. Go back to sleep in the gutter.

(*He flings* THE HUSTLER'S *clothes into the hall.* THE HUSTLER
viciously grabs FLAN *by the lapels of his robe.*)

HUSTLER

Fuck you!

(THE HUSTLER *throws* FLAN *back, picks up his clothes and leaves.* FLAN *catches his breath.* OUISA *is terrified.*)

PAUL

Please. Don't tell my father. I don't want him to know. I haven't told him. He doesn't know. I got so lonely. I got so afraid. My dad coming. I had the money. I went out after we went to sleep and I brought him back. I couldn't be alone. You had so much. I couldn't be alone. I was so afraid.

OUISA

Just go.

PAUL

I'm so sorry.

(PAUL *goes.*
FLAN *and* OUISA, *at a loss, straighten out the pillows on the sofa. They are exhausted.*)

OUISA (*To us*)

And that's that.

FLAN

I am shaking.

OUISA

You have to do *something*!

FLAN

It's awful.

OUISA

Is anything gone?

FLAN

How can I look? I'm shaking.

OUISA

Did he take anything?

FLAN

Would you concentrate on yourself?

OUISA

I want to know if anything's gone?

FLAN

Calm down.

OUISA

We could have been killed.

FLAN

The silver Victorian inkwell.

OUISA

How can you think of *things*? We could have been murdered.

*(An actor appears for a moment holding up an ornate Victorian
inkwell capped by a silver beaver.)*

FLAN

There's the inkwell. Silver beaver. Why?

OUISA

Slashed—our throats slashed.

(Another actor appears for a moment holding up a framed portrait of a dog, say, a pug.)

FLAN

And there's the watercolor. Our dog.

OUISA

Go to bed at night happy and then murdered. Would we have woken up?

FLAN

We're alive.

OUISA

We called our kids.

FLAN

No answer.

(The phone rings. They clutch each other.)

OUISA

It's him!

(FLAN goes to the phone.)

OUISA

Don't pick it up!

(FLAN does.
GEOFFREY *appears.)*

GEOFFREY

Flanders, I'm at the airport. Look, I've been thinking. Those Japs really want the Cezanne. They'll pay. You can depend on me for an additional overcall of two-fifty.

FLAN

Two hundred and fifty thousand?

GEOFFREY

And I was thinking for South Africa. What about a Black American Film Festival? With this Spike Lee you have now and of course get Poitier down to be the president of the jury and I know Cosby and I love this Eddie Murphy and my wife went fishing in Norway with Diana Ross and her new Norwegian husband. And also they must have some *new* blacks—

FLAN

Yes. It sounds a wonderful idea.

GEOFFREY

I'll call him at the Sherry—

FLAN

No! We'll call!

GEOFFREY

They're calling my plane—And again last night—

FLAN

No need to thank. See you shortly.

GEOFFREY

The banks.

FLAN

My lawyer.

GEOFFREY

Exactly.

FLAN

Safe trip.

(GEOFFREY *goes.*
Another couple in their forties, KITTY *and* LARKIN *appear.*
OUISA *and* FLAN *take off their robes and are dressed for day.*)

No one ever enters properly

OUISA

Do we have a story to tell you!

KITTY

Do we have a story to tell *you*!

OUISA *(To us)*

Our two and their son are at Harvard together.

(KITTY *and* LARKIN *are pleased about this.*)

FLAN

Let me tell you our story.

LARKIN

When did your story happen?

FLAN

Last night. We are still zonked.

KITTY

We win. Our story happened Friday night. So we go
first.

LARKIN

We're going to be in the movies.

KITTY

We are going to be in the movie of *Cats.*

(OUISA *and* FLAN *look at each other.*)

OUISA

You tell your story first.

LARKIN

Friday night we were home, the doorbell rang—

KITTY

I am not impressed but it was the son of—

OUISA and FLAN *(To us)*

You got it.

KITTY

The kid was mugged. We had to go out. We left him.
He was so charming. His father was taking the red
eye. He couldn't get into the hotel till seven AM. He
stayed with us.

(*She is very pleased.*)

LARKIN

In the middle of the night, we heard somebody
screaming Burglar! Burglar! We came out in the hall.
Paul is chasing this naked blonde thief down the corri-
dor. The blond thief runs out, the alarm goes off. The
kid saved our lives.

FLAN

That was no burglar.

OUISA

You had another house guest.

(KITTY *and* LARKIN *laugh.*)

LARKIN

We feel so guilty. Paul could've been killed by that intruder. He was very understanding—

OUISA

Was anything missing from your house?

LARKIN

Nothing.

FLAN

Did you give him money?

KITTY

Twenty-five dollars until his father arrived.

FLAN *(To us)*

We told them our story.

KITTY and LARKIN

Oh.

OUISA

Have you talked to your kids?

KITTY

Can't get through.

(OUISA *makes a phone call.*)

PAUL: . . . I never knew I was black in that racist way till I was sixteen and came back here. Very protected. White servants. After the divorce we moved to Switzerland. My mother, brother and I. I don't feel American. I don't even feel black. I suppose that's very lucky for me even though Freud says there's no such thing as luck. Just what you make.

OUISA: Does Freud say that? I think we're lucky having this dinner. Isn't this the finest time? A toast to you.

From left to right, John Cunningham as Flan, James McDaniel as Paul, Stockard Channing as Ouisa and Sam Stoneburner as Geoffrey.

Photo by Brigitte Lacombe.

TRENT: I don't want you to leave me, Paul. I'll go through my address book and tell you about family after family. You'll never not fit in again. We'll give you a new identity. I'll make you the most eagerly sought-after young man in the East. And then I'll come into one of these homes one day—and you'll be there and I'll be presented to you. And I'll pretend to meet you for the first time and our friendship will be witnessed by my friends, our parents' friends. If it all happens under their noses, they can't judge me. They can't disparage you. I'll make you a guest in their houses.

At left, John Cameron Mitchell as Trent with James McDaniel as Paul.

Photo by Brigitte Lacombe.

OUISA: I read somewhere that everybody on this planet is separated by only six other people. . . . I find that A] tremendously comforting that we're so close and B] like Chinese water torture that we're so close. . . . I am bound to everyone on this planet by a trail of six people. It's a profound thought. How Paul found us. . . . How every person is a new door, opening up into other worlds. Six degrees of separation between me and everyone else on this planet.

At left, Stockard Channing as Ouisa and James McDaniel as Paul.

Photo by Brigitte Lacombe.

FLAN: Why does it mean so much to you?

OUISA: He wanted to be us. Everything we are in the world, this paltry thing—our life—he wanted it. He stabbed himself to get in here. He envied us. We're not enough to be envied.

FLAN: Like the papers said. We have hearts.

OUISA: Having a heart is not the point. We were hardly taken in. We believed him—for a few hours. He did more for us in a few hours than our children ever did. He wanted to be your child. Don't let that go. He sat out in that park and said that man is my father. He's in trouble and we don't know how to help him.

From left to right, Stockard Channing as Ouisa, James McDaniel as Paul and John Cunningham as Flan.

Photo by Brigitte Lacombe.

OUISA

Sherry Netherlands. I'd like—

LARKIN *(To us)*

She gave the name.

KITTY

Sidney Poitier must be registered.

(The doorbell rings. FLAN *goes.)*

OUISA

No! I'm not a fan. This is not a fan call. We know he's there. His son is a friend of—

(Click. The Sherry's hung up.)

LARKIN

He must be there under another name.

(Another phone call.)

OUISA

Hi. Celebrity Service? I'm not sure how you work.

KITTY

Greta Garbo used the name Harriet Brown.

OUISA

You track down celebrities? Am I right?

LARKIN

Everybody must have known she was Greta Garbo.

OUISA

I'm trying to find out how one would get in touch with

—No, I'm not a press agent—No, I'm not with anyone
—My husband. Flanders Kittredge. *(Click.)* Celebrity
Service doesn't give out information over the phone.

LARKIN

Try the public library.

KITTY

Try *Who's Who.*

*(FLAN returns carrying an elaborate arrangement of flowers.
FLAN reads the card.)*

FLAN

"To thank you for a wonderful time. Paul Poitier."

(FLAN reaches into the bouquet. He takes out a pot of jam.)

FLAN

A pot of jam?

LARKIN

A pot of jam.

(They back off as if it might explode.)

KITTY

I think we should call the police.

(A DETECTIVE appears.) → immediatly. Not realistic

DETECTIVE

What are the charges?

OUISA

He came into our house.

FLAN

He cooked us dinner.

OUISA

He told us the story of *Catcher in the Rye*.

FLAN

He said he was the son of Sidney Poitier.

DETECTIVE

Was he?

OUISA

We don't know.

FLAN

We gave him fifty dollars.

KITTY

We gave him twenty-five.

LARKIN

Shhhh!

OUISA

He picked up a hustler.

FLAN

He left.

KITTY

He chased the burglar out of our house.

OUISA

He didn't steal anything.

LARKIN

We looked and looked.

KITTY

Top to bottom. Nothing gone.

(THE DETECTIVE *closes his notebook.*)

OUISA

Granted this does not seem major now.

DETECTIVE

Look. We're very busy.

FLAN

You can't chuck us out.

DETECTIVE

Come up with charges. Then I'll do something.

(THE DETECTIVE *goes.*)

OUISA *(To us)*

Our kids came down from Harvard.

(Their children, WOODY *and* TESS, *and* KITTY *and* LARKIN'S *boy,* BEN, *enter, groaning.)*

FLAN

—the details he knew—how would he know about the painting? Although I think it's a very fine Kandinsky.

OUISA

And none of you know this fellow? He has this wild quality—yet a real elegance and a real concern and a real consideration—

TESS

Well, Mom, you should have let him stay. You should have divorced all your children and just let this dreamboat stay. Plus he sent you flowers.

FLAN

And jam.

THE KIDS

Oooooo.

OUISA

I wish I knew how to get hold of his father. Just to see if there is any truth in it.

LARKIN

Who knows Sidney Poitier so we could just call him up and ask him?

KITTY *(Eager)*

I have a friend who does theatrical law. I bet he—

LARKIN

What friend?

KITTY

Oh, it's nobody.

LARKIN

I want to know.

KITTY *(Screams)*

Nobody!

LARKIN

Whatever's going on anywhere, I do not want to know.

I don't want to know. I don't want to know...

KITTY *(Overlapping)*

Nobody. Nobody. Nobody...

BEN

Dad. Mom. Please. For once. Please?

(BEN, KITTY, LARKIN *go in anguish.*)

FLAN

Tess, when you see your little sister, don't tell her that he and the, uh, hustler, used her bed.

TESS

You put him in that bed. I'm not going to get involved with any conspiracy.

FLAN

It's not a conspiracy. It's a *family*.

(TESS *and* FLAN *growl at each other.*
Darkness.
OUISA, *alone, stretches out on the sofa.*
PAUL *appears wearing the pink shirt.*)

PAUL

The imagination. That's our out. Our imagination teaches us our limits and then how to grow beyond those limits. The imagination says Listen to me. I am your darkest voice. I am your 4 AM voice. I am the voice that wakes you up and says this is what I'm afraid of. Do not listen to me at your peril. The imagination is the noon voice that sees clearly and says yes, this is what I want for my life. It's there to sort out your nightmare, to show you the exit from the maze of your nightmare, to transform the nightmare into dreams that become your bedrock. If we don't listen to that voice, it dies. It shrivels. It vanishes.

(PAUL *takes out a switchblade and opens it.*)

The imagination is not our escape. On the contrary, the imagination is the place we are all trying to get to.

(PAUL *lifts his shirt and stabs himself.*
OUISA *sits up and screams.*
PAUL *is gone.*
The phone rings. It's THE DETECTIVE.)

DETECTIVE
I got a call that might interest you.

(DR. FINE *appears, a very earnest professional man in his 50s.*)

DR. FINE *(To us)*
I was seeing a patient. I'm an obstetrician at New York Hospital. The nurse opened my office door and said there's a friend of your son's here...

(PAUL *appears.*)

DR. FINE *(To us)*
I treated the kid. He was more scared than hurt. A knife wound, a few bruises.

PAUL
I don't know how to thank you, sir. My father is coming here.

(*The four parents appear.*)

FLAN and OUISA and KITTY and LARKIN
He's making a film of *Cats*.

DR. FINE
And he told me the name of a matinee idol of my
youth. Somebody who had really forged ahead and
made new paths for blacks just by the strength of his
own talent. Strangely, I had identified with him before
I started medical school. I mean, I'm a Jew. My grandparents were killed in the war. I had this sense of self-
hatred, of fear. And this kid's father—the bravery of
his films—had given me a direction, a confidence.
Simple as that. We're always paying off debts.

Then my beeper went off. A patient in her tenth
month of labor. Her water finally broke. I gave him the
keys.

(PAUL *catches the keys.*)

PAUL
Doug told me all about your brownstone. How you got
it at a great price because there had been a murder in it
and for a while people thought it had a curse but you
were a scientific man and were courageous!

DR. FINE
Well, yes! Courageous!
I ran off to the delivery room. Twins! Two boys.
I thought of my son. I dialed my boy at Dartmouth.
Amazingly, he was in his room. Doing *what* I hate to
ask.

(DOUG, 20, *appears.*)

DR. FINE
So you accuse me of having no interest in your life,

not doing for friends, being a rotten father. Well, you should be very happy.

DOUG

The son of who? Dad, I never heard of him. Dad, as usual, you are a real cretin. You gave him the keys? You gave a complete stranger who happens to mention my name the keys to our house? Dad, sometimes it is so obvious to me why Mom left. I am so embarrassed to know you. You gave the keys to a stranger who shows up at your office? Mother told me you beat her! Mom told me you were a rotten lover and drank so much your body smelled of cheap white wine. Mom said sleeping with you was like sleeping with a salad made of bad dressing. Why you had to bring me into the world!

DR. FINE

There are two sides to every story—

DOUG

You're an idiot! You're an idiot!

(DOUG *goes into the dark, screaming.*)

DR. FINE

I went home—courageously—with a policeman.

(A POLICEMAN *accompanies* DR. FINE. PAUL *appears wearing a silk robe, carrying a snifter of brandy.*)

DR. FINE

Arrest him!

PAUL

Pardon?

DR. FINE

Breaking and entering.

PAUL

Breaking and entering?

DR. FINE

You're an imposter.

PAUL

Officer, your honor, your eminence, Dr. Fine *gave* me the keys to his brownstone. Isn't that so?

DR. FINE

My son doesn't know you.

PAUL

This man gave me the keys to the house. Isn't that so?

POLICEMAN (*Screams*)

Did you give him the key to the house?

DR. FINE

Yes! But under false pretenses. This fucking black kid crack addict came into my office lying—

PAUL

I have taken this much brandy but can pour the rest back into the bottle. And I've used electricity listening to the music, but I think you'll find that nothing's taken from the house.

(PAUL *goes*.)

DR. FINE

I want you to arrest this fraud.

(The POLICEMAN *walks away.*
DOUG *returns.)*

DOUG
A cretin. A creep! No wonder mother left you!

*(*DOUG *goes.*
Pause.)

DR. FINE
Two sides. Every story.

*(*OUISA *holds up a book.)*

OUISA
I went down to the Strand. I got Sidney Poitier's autobiography. *(Reads:)* "Back in New York with Juanita
and the children, I began to become aware that our
marriage, while working on some levels, was falling
apart in other fundamental areas."

FLAN
There's a picture of him and his four—daughters. No
sons. Four daughters. The book's called *This Life*.

DR. FINE
Published by Knopf.

KITTY
1980.

LARKIN
Out of print.

KITTY
Oh dear.

OUISA

This kid bulldozing his way into our lives.

LARKIN

We let him in our lives. I run a foundation. You're a dealer. You're a doctor. You'd think we'd be satisfied with our achievements.

FLAN

Agatha Christie would ask, what do we all have in common?

OUISA

It seems the common thread linking us all is an overwhelming need to be in the movie of *Cats*.

KITTY

Our kids. Struggling through their lives.

LARKIN

I don't want to know anything about the spillover of their lives.

OUISA

All we have in common is our children went to boarding school together.

FLAN *(To* DR. FINE*)*

How come we never met?

DR. FINE

His mother had custody. I lived out West. After he graduated from high school, she moved West. I moved East.

LARKIN

I think we should drop it right here.

KITTY

Are you afraid Ben is mixed up in this fraud?

LARKIN

I don't want to know too much about my kid.

KITTY

You think Ben is hiding things from us? I tell you, I'm getting to the bottom of this. My son has no involvements with any black frauds. Doctor, you said something about crack?

LARKIN

I don't want to know.

DR. FINE

It just leaped out of my mouth. No proof. Oh dear god, no proof.

FLAN

We'll take a vote. Do we pursue this to the end no matter what we find out about our kids?

OUISA

I vote yes.

DR. FINE

I trust Doug. Yes.

LARKIN

No.

KITTY

Yes.

FLAN

Yes.

(KITTY *looks through the Poitier autobiography.*)

KITTY

Listen to the last page. "...making it better for our children. Protecting them. From what? The truth is what we were protecting those little people from... there is a lot to worry about and I'd better start telling the little bastards—start worrying!" The end.

(KITTY *closes the book in dismay. All the children,* TESS, WOODY, BEN, DOUG, *enter, groaning.*)

FLAN

It's obvious. It's somebody you went to high school with, since you each go to different colleges.

OUISA

He knows the details about our lives.

FLAN

Who in your high school, part of your gang, has become homosexual or is deep into drugs?

TESS

That's like, about fifteen people.

LARKIN

I don't want to know.

TESS

I find it really insulting that you would assume that it has to be a guy. This movie star's son could have had a relationship with a girl in high school—

BEN

That's your problem in a nutshell. You're so limited.

TESS

That's why I'm going to Afghanistan. To climb mountains.

OUISA

You are not climbing mountains.

FLAN

We have not invested all this money in you to scale the face of K–2.

TESS

Is that all I am? An investment?

OUISA

All right. Track down everybody in your high school class. Male. Female. Whatever. Not just homosexuals. Drug addicts. The kid might be a drug dealer.

DOUG

Why do you look at me when you say that? Do you think I'm an addict? A drug pusher? I really resent the accusations.

DR. FINE

No one is accusing you of anything.

LARKIN

I don't want to know. I don't want to know. I don't want
to know.

FLAN

Nobody is accusing anyone of anything. I'm asking
you to go on a detective search and find out from your
high school class if anyone has met a black kid pre-
tending to be a movie star's son.

BEN

He promised you parts in *Cats*?

OUISA

It wasn't just that. It was fun.

TESS

You went to *Cats*. You said it was an all-time low in a
lifetime of theater-going.

OUISA

Film is a different medium.

TESS

You said Aeschylus did not invent theater to have it
end up a bunch of chorus kids wondering which of
them will go to Kitty Kat Heaven.

OUISA

I don't remember saying that.

FLAN

No, I think that was *Starlight Express*—

TESS

Well, maybe he'll make a movie of *Starlight Express* and

you can all be on roller skates—

DOUG

This is so humiliating.

BEN

This is so pathetic.

TESS

This is so racist.

OUISA

This is *not* racist!

DOUG

How can I get in touch with anybody in high school? I've outgrown them.

KITTY

How can you outgrow them? You graduated a year ago!

OUISA

Here is a copy of your yearbook. I want you to get the phone numbers of everybody in your class. You all went to the same boarding school. You can phone from here.

DR. FINE

You can charge it to my phone.

OUISA

Call everyone in your class and ask them if they know—

DOUG

Never!

TESS

This is the KGB.

DR. FINE

You're on the phone all the time. Now I ask you to make calls all over the country and you become reticent.

TESS

This is the entire McCarthy period.

WOODY

I just want to get one thing straight.

FLAN

Finally, we hear from the peanut gallery.

WOODY

You gave him my pink shirt? You gave a complete stranger my pink shirt? That pink shirt was a Christmas present from *you*. I treasured that shirt. I loved that shirt. My collar size has grown a full size from weight lifting. And you saw my arms had grown, you saw my neck had grown. And you bought me that shirt for my new body. I loved that shirt. The first shirt for my new body. And you gave that shirt away. I can't believe it. I hate it here. I hate this house. I hate you.

DOUG

You never do anything for me.

TESS

You've never done anything but tried to block me.

BEN

I'm only this pathetic extension of your eighth-rate

personality.

DOUG

Social Darwinism pushed beyond all limits.

WOODY

You gave away my pink shirt?

TESS

You want me to be everything you weren't.

DOUG

You said drugs and looked at me.

(The parents leave, speechless, defeated. The kids look through their high school yearbook. TESS *spots a face.)*

TESS

Trent Conway.

ALL THE KIDS

Trent Conway.

(TRENT CONWAY appears.)

TESS

Trent Conway. Look at those beady eyes staring out at me. Trent Conway. He's at MIT.

(To us)

So I went to MIT. He was there in his computer room and I just pressed him and pressed him and pressed him. I had a tape recorder strapped to me.

(Darkness)

TRENT'S VOICE TAPED
Yes, I knew Paul.

TESS'S VOICE TAPED
But what happened between you?

TRENT'S VOICE TAPED
It was...It was...

(*The lights come up slowly.* PAUL *and* TRENT *appear. Rain. Distant thunder. Jazz playing somewhere off.* PAUL *is dressed in jeans and a tank top, high-top sneakers.*)

TRENT
This is the way you must speak. Hear my accent. Hear my voice. Never say you're going horse-back riding. You say you're going riding. And don't say couch. Say sofa. And you say *bodd*-ill. It's bottle. Say bottle of beer.

PAUL
Bodd-ill a bee-ya.

TRENT
Bottle of beer.

(PAUL *sits on the sofa. He pulls out a thick address book from under him.*)

PAUL
What's this?

TRENT
My address book.

PAUL

All these names. Addresses. Tell me about these people.

(TRENT *sits beside him.*)

TRENT

I want you to come to bed with me.

PAUL *(Fierce)*

Tell me about these people, man!

TRENT

I just want to look at you. Sorry.

(PAUL *is hypnotized by the address book.*)

PAUL

Are these all rich people?

TRENT

No. Hand to mouth on a higher plateau.

PAUL

I think it must be very hard to be with rich people. You have to have money. You have to give them presents.

TRENT

Not at all. Rich people do something nice for you, you give them a pot of jam.

PAUL

That's what pots of jam are for?

TRENT

Orange. Grapefruit. Strawberry. But fancy. They have

entire stores filled with fancy pots of jam wrapped in cloth. English. Or French.

PAUL

I'll tell you what I'll do. I pick a name. You tell me about them. Where they live. Secrets. And for each name you get a piece of clothing.

TRENT

All right.

PAUL

Kittredge. Talbot and Woodrow.

TRENT

Talbot, called Tess, was anorexic and was in a hospital for a while.

(PAUL *takes off a shoe and kicks it to* TRENT.)

PAUL

Their parents.

TRENT

Ouisa and Flan, for Flanders, Kittredge. Rhode Island, I believe. Newport, but not along the ocean. The street behind the ocean. He's an art dealer. They have a Kandinsky.

PAUL

A Kan—what—ski?

TRENT

Kandinsky. A double-sided Kandinsky.

(PAUL *kicks off his other shoe.* TRENT *catches it joyously.*)

TRENT

I feel like Scheherazade!

(*He embraces* PAUL *with fierce tenderness.*)

I don't want you to leave me, Paul. I'll go through my
address book and tell you about family after family.
You'll never not fit in again. We'll give you a new identity. I'll make you the most eagerly sought-after young
man in the East. And then I'll come into one of these
homes one day—and you'll be there and I'll be presented to you. And I'll pretend to meet you for the
first time and our friendship will be witnessed by my
friends, our parents' friends. If it all happens under
their noses, they can't judge me. They can't disparage
you. I'll make you a guest in their houses. Ask me
another name. I'd like to try for the shirt.

(PAUL *kisses* TRENT.)

PAUL

That's enough for today.

(PAUL *takes his shoes and the address book and goes.*
TRENT *turns to* TESS.)

TRENT

Paul stayed with me for three months. We went
through the address book letter by letter. Paul vanished by the L's. He took the address book with him.
Well, he's already been in all your houses. Maybe I
will meet him again. I sure would like to.

TESS

His past? His real name?

TRENT

I don't know anything about him. It was a rainy night in Boston. He was in a doorway. That's all.

TESS

He took stuff from you?

TRENT

Besides the address book? He took my stereo and sport jacket and my word processor and my laser printer. And my skis. And my TV.

TESS

Will you press charges?

TRENT

No.

TESS

It's a felony.

TRENT

Why do they want to find him?

TESS

They say to help him. If there's a crime, the cops will get involved.

TRENT

Look, we must keep in touch. We were friends for a brief bit in school. I mean we were really good friends.

TESS

Won't you press charges?

TRENT

Please.

(They go.
OUISA *appears.)*

> OUISA *(To us)*

Tess played me the tapes.

> TESS'S VOICE TAPED

Won't you press charges?

> TRENT'S VOICE TAPED

Please.

> OUISA *(To us)*

Can you believe it? Paul learned all that in three months. Three months! Who would have thought it? Trent Conway, the Henry Higgins of our time. Paul looked at those names and said I am Columbus. I am Magellan. I will sail into this new world.

I read somewhere that everybody on this planet is separated by only six other people. Six degrees of separation. Between us and everybody else on this planet. The president of the United States. A gondolier in Venice. Fill in the names. I find that A] tremendously comforting that we're so close and B] like Chinese water torture that we're so close. Because you have to find the right six people to make the connection. It's not just big names. It's *anyone*. A native in a rain forest. A Tierra del Fuegan. An Eskimo. I am bound to everyone on this planet by a trail of six people. It's a profound thought. How Paul found us. How to find the man whose son he pretends to be. Or perhaps *is* his son, although I doubt it. How every person is a new door, opening up into other worlds. Six degrees of separation between me and everyone else on this planet. But to find the right six people.

(FLAN *appears.*)

> FLAN (*To us*)
> We didn't hear for a while. We went about our lives.

(*The* DOORMAN *appears.*)

> OUISA (*To us*)
> And then one day our doorman, whom we tip very well at Christmas and any time he does something nice for us—our doorman spit at my husband, J. Flanders Kittredge. I mean, spit at him.

(*The* DOORMAN *spits at* FLAN.)

> DOORMAN
> Your son! I know all about your son.

> FLAN
> What about my son?

> DOORMAN
> Not the little shit who lives here. The other son. The secret son. The Negro son you deny.

(*The* DOORMAN *spits at* FLAN *again.*)

> FLAN
> The Negro son?

> DOORMAN
> The black son you make live in Central Park.

> OUISA (*To us*)
> The next chapter. Rick and Elizabeth and Paul sit on the grass in Central Park.

(RICK, ELIZABETH *and* PAUL *run on laughing in Central Park.*
RICK, *a nice young guy in his mid-twenties, plays the guitar ener-*
getically. He and PAUL *and* ELIZABETH, *a beautiful girl in her mid-*
twenties, are having a great time singing a cheery song, say James
Taylor's "Shower The People," until RICK *hits the wrong chord. They*
try to break down the harmony. RICK *can't for the life of him find the*
right chord. THE THREE OF THEM *laugh.* PAUL *is wearing the pink*
shirt.)

PAUL
Tell me about yourselves.

RICK
We're here from Utah.

PAUL
Do they have any black people in Utah?

RICK
Maybe two. Yes, the Mormons brought in two.

ELIZABETH
We came to be actors.

RICK
She won the all-state competition for comedy and
drama.

PAUL
My gosh!

ELIZABETH
"The quality of mercy is not strained.
It droppeth like the gentle rain from heaven."

RICK
And we study and we wait tables.

ELIZABETH

Because you have to have technique.

PAUL

Like the painters. Cezanne looked for the rules behind the spontaneity of Impressionism.

RICK

Cez—That's a painter?

ELIZABETH

We don't know anything about painting.

PAUL

My dad loves painting. He has a Kandinsky but he loves Cezanne the most. He lives up there.

RICK

What?

PAUL

He lives up there. Count six windows over. John Flanders Kittredge. His chums call him Flan. I was the child of Flan's hippie days. His radical days. He went down South as a freedom marcher, to register black voters—his friends were killed. Met my mother. Registered her and married her in a fit of sentimental righteousness and knocked her up with me and came back here and abandoned her. Went to Harvard. He's now a fancy art dealer. Lives up there. Count six windows over. Won't see me. The new wife—the white wife—The Louisa Kittredge Call Me Ouisa Wife—the mother of the new children wife—

RICK

Your brothers and sisters?

PAUL *(Bitter)*

They go to Andover and Exeter and Harvard and Yale. The awful thing is my father started out good. My mother says there is a good man inside J. Flanders Kittredge.

ELIZABETH

He'll see you if he was that good. He can't forget you entirely.

PAUL

I call him. He hangs up.

RICK

Go to his office—

PAUL

He doesn't have an office. He works out of there. They won't even let me in the elevator.

RICK

Dress up as a messenger.

ELIZABETH

Say you have a masterpiece for him. "I got the Mona Lisa waitin' out in the truck."

PAUL

I don't want to embarrass him. Look, this is so fucking tacky. *(Pause)* You love each other?

ELIZABETH

A lot.

(RICK *and* ELIZABETH *touch each other's hands.)*

PAUL

I hope we can meet again.

(PAUL *turns to go.*)

RICK

Where do you live?

PAUL

Live? I'm home.

ELIZABETH

You're not out on the streets?

PAUL

You're such assholes. Where would I live?

RICK

Stay with us.

ELIZABETH

We just have a railroad flat in a tenement—

RICK

It's over a roller disco. The last of the roller discos but it's quiet by five AM and a great narrow space—

ELIZABETH

A railroad loft and we could give you a corner. The tub's in the kitchen but there's light in the morning—

RICK (*To us*)

And he did!

(*The light changes to the loft.*)

PAUL

This is the way you must speak. Hear my accent. Hear my voice. Never say you're going horse-back riding. You say you're going riding. And don't say couch. Say sofa. And you say bodd-ill. It's bottle. Say bottle of beer.

RICK

Bodd-ill a bee-ya.

PAUL

Bottle of beer. And never be afraid of rich people You know what they love? A fancy pot of jam. That's all. Get yourself a patron. That's what you need. You shouldn't be waiting tables. You're going to wake up one day and the temporary job you picked up to stay alive is going to be your full-time life.

(ELIZABETH *embraces* PAUL *gratefully.*)

PAUL

You've given me courage. I'm going to try and see him right now.

(PAUL *goes.*

RICK *and* ELIZABETH *lay on their backs and dream.*)

RICK

I'll tell you all the parts I want to do. Vanya in *Uncle Vanya*.

ELIZABETH

Masha in *Three Sisters*. No, Irina first. The young one who yearns for love. Then Masha who loves. Then the oldest one, Olga, who never knows love.

RICK

I'd like a shot at Laertes. I think it's a much better part.

(ELIZABETH *gazes in a mirror.*)

ELIZABETH

Do you think it'll hurt me?

RICK

What'll hurt you?

ELIZABETH

My resemblance to Liv Ullmann.

(PAUL *runs in.*)

PAUL

HE WROTE ME! I WROTE HIM AND HE WROTE ME
BACK!!! He's going to give me a thousand dollars! And
that's just for starters! He sold a Cezanne to the Japanese and made millions and he can give me money
without her knowing it.

ELIZABETH

I knew it!

PAUL

I'm moving out of here!

ELIZABETH

You can't!

RICK

No!

PAUL

But I am going to give you the money to put on a

showcase of any play you want and you'll be in it and agents will come see you and you'll be seen and you'll be started. And when you win your Oscars—both of you—you'll look in the camera and thank me—

ELIZABETH

I want to thank Paul Kittredge.

RICK

Thanks, Paul!

PAUL

One hitch. I'm going to meet him in Maine. He's up there visiting his parents in Dark Harbor. My grandparents whom I've never met. He's finally going to tell my grandparents about me. He's going to make up for lost time. He's going to give me money. I can go back home. Get my momma that beauty parlor she's wanted all her life. One problem. How am I going to get to Maine? The wife checks all the bills. He has to account for the money. She handles the purse strings. Where the hell am I going to get two hundred and fifty dollars to get to Maine?

ELIZABETH

How long would you need it for?

PAUL

I'll be gone a week. But I could wire it back to you.

RICK (*Quiet*)

We could lend it to him for a week.

ELIZABETH (*Quiet*)

We can't. If something happens—

RICK *(Quiet)*
You're like his stepmother. These women holding on
to all the purse strings.

ELIZABETH
No. We worked too hard to save that. I'm sorry.
I'll meet you both after work. If your father loves you,
he'll get you the ticket up there.

(She goes.)

RICK *(To us)*
We stopped by the bank. I withdrew the money. He
took it.

PAUL
Let's celebrate!
(ELIZABETH *appears.*)

ELIZABETH *(To us)*
I went to a money machine to get twenty dollars and I
couldn't get anything. The machine devoured my
card. I called up the emergency number and the voice
said my account was closed. They had withdrawn all
the money and closed the account. I went to that
apartment on Fifth Avenue. I told the doorman: I want
my money. I work tables. I work hard. I saved. I'm here
trying to get to meet people. I am stranded. Who do I
know to go to? "The quality of mercy is not strained?"
Fuck you, quality of mercy.

(She goes.
RICK *appears.)*

RICK *(To us)*
He told me he had some of his own money and he

wanted to treat me. We went to a store that rented tuxedos and we dressed to the nines. We went to the Rainbow Room. We danced. High over New York City. I swear. He stood up and held out my chair and we danced and there was a stir. Nothing like this ever happened in Utah. And we danced. And I'll tell you nothing like that must have ever happened at the Rainbow Room because we were asked to leave. I tell you. It was so funny.

And we walked out and walked home and I knew Elizabeth was waiting for me and I would have to explain about the money and calm her down because we'll get it back but I forgot because we took a carriage ride in the park and he asked me if he could fuck me and I had never done anything like that and he did and it was fantastic. It was the greatest night I ever had and before we got home he kissed me on the mouth and he vanished.

Later I realized he had no money of his own. He had spent my money—our money—on that night at the Rainbow Room.

How am I going to face Elizabeth? What have I done? What did I let him do to me? I wanted experience. I came here to have experience. But I didn't come here to do this or lose that or be this or do this to Elizabeth. I didn't come here to be *this*. My father said I was a fool and I can't have him be right. What have I done?

(He goes into the dark.
LARKIN *and* KITTY *appear.)*

LARKIN
Kitty and I were at a roller disco two clients opened.

KITTY

And it was Valentine's Day

LARKIN

and we came out and we saw a body on the street.

KITTY

My legs were still shaky from the roller skating which
I have not done in I hate to tell you how many years
and we knew the body had just landed there in that
clump

LARKIN

because the blood seeping out had not reached the
gutter yet.

KITTY

You could see the blood just oozing out slowly
towards the curb.

LARKIN

The boy had jumped from above.

KITTY

The next day we walked through the park by Gracie
Mansion

LARKIN

and it was cold and we saw police putting a jacket on a
man sitting on a bench.

KITTY

Only we got closer and it wasn't a sweater.

LARKIN

It was a body bag. A homeless person had frozen during the night.

KITTY

Was it that cold?

LARKIN

Sometimes there are periods where you see death everywhere.

(Darkness. OUISA *and* FLAN *appear in their robes with* THE DETECTIVE *and* ELIZABETH.*)*

DETECTIVE

This young girl came forward with the story. She told me the black kid was your son, lived here. It all seemed to come into place. What I'm saying is she'll press charges.

ELIZABETH

I want him dead. He took all our money. He took my life. Rick's dead! You bet your life I'll press charges.

OUISA

We haven't seen him since that night.

DETECTIVE

Find him. We have a case.

FLAN

I'll release it to the papers. I have friends. I can call the *Times.*

OUISA *(To us)*

Which is what happened.

FLAN *(To us)*

The paper of note—the *Times*—ran a story on so-called smart, sophisticated, tough New Yorkers being boondoggled by a confidence man now wanted by the

police. Who says New Yorkers don't have a heart?
They promised it would either run in the Living section or the Home section.

KITTY *(To us)*

The story ran.

DR. FINE *(To us)*

In the B section front page.

DETECTIVE *(To us)*

Smart New Yorkers.

LARKIN *(To us)*

We never heard from Sidney Poitier.

OUISA *(To us)*

Six degrees. Six degrees.

(They all go except for OUISA *and* FLAN, *who pull off their robes,
they are dressing for the evening.)*

OUISA *(To us)*

We are bidding tonight on an Henri Matisse.

FLAN *(To us)*

We will go as high as—

OUISA

Don't tell all the family secrets—

FLAN *(To us)*

Well over twenty-five million.

OUISA *(To us)*

Out of which he will keep—

FLAN *(To us)*

I'll have to give most of it away, but the good part is it
gives me a credibility in this new market. I mean, a
David fucking Hockney print sold for a hundred
bucks fifteen years ago went for thirty-four thousand
dollars! A print! A flower. You know Geoffrey. Our
South African—

OUISA *(To us)*

—it's a black-tie auction—Sotheby's—

FLAN

I know we'll get it.

OUISA *(Noting the time)*

Flan—

FLAN

I know the Matisse will be mine—for a few hours.
Then off to Tokyo. Or Saudi.

(FLAN leaves as OUISA phones TESS.)

OUISA *(To TESS)*

I'm totally dolled up. The black. Have you seen it? I
have to tell you the sign I saw today. Cruelty-free cosmetics. A store was selling cruelty-free cosmetics.

TESS

Mother, that is such a beautiful thing. Do you realize
the agony cosmetic companies put rabbits through to
test eye shadow?

OUISA

Dearest, I know that. I'm only talking about the
phrase. Cruelty-free cosmetics should take away all

evidence of time and cellulite and—

TESS

Mother, I'm getting married.

OUISA

I thought you were going to Afghanistan.

TESS

I am going to get married and then go to Afghanistan.

OUISA

One country at a time. You are not getting married.

TESS

Immediately so deeply negative—

OUISA

I know everyone you know and you are not marrying any of them.

TESS

The arrogance that you would assume you know everyone I know. The way you say it: I know everyone you know—

OUISA

Unless you met them in the last two days—you can't hold a secret.

(The other line rings.)

Wait—I'm putting you on hold—

TESS

No one ever calls on that number.

OUISA

Wait. Hold on.

TESS

Mother!

OUISA

Hello?

(PAUL *appears, frightened.*)

PAUL

Hello.

OUISA

Paul?

PAUL

I saw the story in the paper. I didn't know the boy killed himself. He gave me the money.

OUISA

Let me put you on hold. I'm talking to my child—

PAUL

If you put me on hold, I'll be gone and you'll never hear from me again.

(OUISA *pauses.* TESS *fades into black.*)

OUISA

You have to turn yourself in. The boy committed suicide. You stole the money. The girl is pressing charges. They're going to get you. Why not turn yourself in and you can get off easier. You can strike a bargain. Learn when you're trapped. You're so brilliant. You have such promise. You need help.

PAUL

Would you help me?

OUISA

What would you want me to do?

PAUL

Stay with you.

OUISA

That's impossible.

PAUL

Why?

OUISA

My husband feels you betrayed him.

PAUL

Do you?

OUISA

You were lunatic! And picking that drek off the street. Are you suicidal? Do you have AIDS? Are you infected?

PAUL

I do not have it. It's a miracle. But I don't. Do you feel I betrayed you? If you do, I'll hang up and never bother you again—

OUISA

Where have you been?

PAUL

Travelling.

OUISA

You're not in trouble? I mean, more trouble?

PAUL

No, I only visited you. I didn't like the first people so much. They went out and just left me alone. I didn't like the doctor. He was too eager to please. And he left me alone. But you. You and your husband. We all stayed together.

OUISA

What did you want from us?

PAUL

Everlasting friendship.

OUISA

Nobody has that.

PAUL

You do.

OUISA

What do you think we are?

PAUL

You're going to tell me secrets? You're not what you appear to be? You have no secrets. Trent Conway told me what your kids have told him over the years.

OUISA

What have the kids told him about us?

PAUL

I don't tell that. I save that for blackmail.

OUISA

Then perhaps I'd better hang up.

PAUL *(Panic)*

No! I went to a museum! I liked Toulouse-Lautrec!

OUISA

As well you should.

PAUL

I read *The Andy Warhol Diaries*.

OUISA

Ahh, you've become an aesthete.

PAUL

Are you laughing at me?

OUISA

No. I read them too.

PAUL

I read *The Agony and the Ecstasy*, by Irving Stone, about Michelangelo painting the Sistine Chapel.

OUISA

You're ahead of me there.

PAUL

Have you seen the Sistine Chapel?

OUISA

Oh yes. Even gone to the top of it in a rickety elevator to watch the men clean it.

PAUL

You've been to the top of the Sistine Chapel?

OUISA

Absolutely. Stood right under the hand of God touching the hand of man. The workman said "Hit it. Hit it. It's only a fresco." I did. I slapped God's hand.

PAUL

You did?

OUISA

And you know what they clean it with? All this technology. Q-tips and water.

PAUL

No!

OUISA

Clean away the years of grime and soot and paintovers. Q-tips and water changing the history of Western Art. Vivid colors.

PAUL

Take me to see it?

OUISA

Take you to see it? Paul, they think you might have murdered someone! You stole money!

(FLAN *appears, needing help with his studs.*)

FLAN

Honey, could you give me a hand with—

OUISA (*Mouths to* FLAN)

It's Paul.

(FLAN *goes to the other phone.*)

FLAN

I'll call that detective.

(The other line rings. TESS *appears.)*

TESS

Dad! We were cut off. I'm getting marr—

FLAN

Darling, could you call back—

TESS

I'm getting married and going to Afghanistan—

FLAN

We cannot talk about this now—

TESS

I'm going to ruin my life and get married and throw away everything you want me to be because it's the only way to hurt you!

*(*TESS *goes.*
THE DETECTIVE *appears.)*

FLAN

I've got that kid on the line.

DETECTIVE

Find out where he is.

*(*THE DETECTIVE *goes.)*

FLAN *(Mouths to* OUISA*)*

Find out where he is???

PAUL

Who's there?

OUISA

Look, why don't you come here. Where are you?

PAUL

I come there and you'll have the cops waiting.

OUISA

You have to trust us.

PAUL

Why?

OUISA

Because—we like you.

FLAN *(Mouths)*

Where is he?

PAUL

Who's there?

OUISA

It's—

FLAN

I'm not here.

OUISA

It's Flan.

PAUL

Are you in tonight? I could come and make a feast for
you.

OUISA

We're going out now. But you could be here when we
come back.

FLAN

Are you nuts! Tell a crook we're going out. The house
is empty.

PAUL

Where are you going?

OUISA

To Sotheby's.

(FLAN *grabs the phone.*)

FLAN

The key's under the mat!

PAUL

Hi! Can I come to Sotheby's?

(FLAN *hands the phone back to* OUISA.)

OUISA

Hi.

PAUL

I said hi to Flan.

OUISA

Paul says hi.

FLAN

Hi.

OUISA

Sotheby's.

PAUL

That's wonderful! I'll come!

OUISA

You can't.

PAUL

Why? I was helpful last time—

FLAN

Thank him—he was very help—

(OUISA *hands* FLAN *the phone.*)

FLAN

Paul? You were helpful getting me this contract—

PAUL

Really! I was thinking maybe that's what I should do is what you do—in art but making money out of art and meeting people and not working in an office—

FLAN

You only see the glam side of it. There's a whole grotty side that—

PAUL

I could learn the grotty—

FLAN

You have to have art history. You have to have language. You have to have economics—

PAUL

I'm fast. I could do it. Do your kids want to—

FLAN

No, it's not really a profession you hand down from
generation to gen—what the hell am I talking career
counselling to you! You embarrassed me in my building! You stole money. There is a warrant out for your
arrest!

(OUISA *wrests the phone away.*)

OUISA

Don't hang up! PAUL? Are you there? PAUL? *(To* FLAN*)*
You made him hang up—

PAUL

I'm here.

OUISA

You are! Who are you? What's your real name?

PAUL

If you let me stay with you, I'll tell you. That night was
the happiest night I ever had.

OUISA *(To* FLAN*)*

It was the happiest night he ever had.

FLAN

Oh please. I am not a bullshitter but never bullshit a
bullshitter.

(FLAN *goes.*)

OUISA

Why?

PAUL

You let me use all the parts of myself that night—

OUISA

It was magical. That Salinger stuff—

PAUL

Graduation speech at Groton two years ago.

OUISA

Your cooking—

PAUL

Other people's recipes. Did you see Donald Barthelme's obituary? He said collage was the art form of the twentieth century.

OUISA

Everything is somebody else's.

PAUL

Not your children. Not your life.

OUISA

Yes. You got me there. That is mine. It is no one else's.

PAUL

You don't sound happy.

OUISA

There's so much you don't know. You are so smart and so stupid—

PAUL *(Furious)*

Never say I'm stupid—

OUISA

Have some flexibility. You're stupid not to recognize what you could be.

PAUL

What could I be?

OUISA

So much.

PAUL

With you behind me?

OUISA

Perhaps. You liked that night? I've thought since that you spent all your time laughing at us.

PAUL

No.

OUISA

That you had brought that awful hustling thing back to show us your contempt—

PAUL

I was so happy. I wanted to add sex to it. Don't you do that?

(Pause)

OUISA

No.

PAUL

I'll tell you my name.

OUISA

Please?

PAUL

It's Paul Poitier-Kittredge. It's a hyphenated name.

(*Pause*)

OUISA

Paul, you need help. Go to the police. Turn yourself in.
You'll be over it all the sooner. You can start.

PAUL

Start what?

OUISA

Your life.

PAUL

Will you help me?

(OUISA *pauses, and makes a decision.*)

OUISA

I will help you. But you have to go to the police and go
to jail and—

PAUL

Will you send me books and polaroids of you and cas-
settes? And letters?

OUISA

Yes.

PAUL

Will you visit me?

OUISA

I will visit you.

PAUL

And when you do, you'll wear your best clothes and knock em dead?

OUISA

I'll knock em dead. But you've got to be careful in prison. You have to use condoms.

PAUL

I won't have sex in prison. I only have sex when I'm happy.

OUISA

Go to the police.

PAUL

Will you take me?

OUISA

I'll give you the name of the detective to see—

PAUL

I'll be treated with care if you take me to the police. If they don't know you're special, they kill you.

OUISA

I don't think they kill you.

PAUL

Mrs. Louisa Kittredge, I am black.

OUISA

I will deliver you to them with kindness and affection.

PAUL

And I'll plead guilty and go to prison and serve a few months.

OUISA

A few months tops.

PAUL

Then I'll come out and work for you and learn—

OUISA

We'll work that out.

PAUL

I want to know now.

OUISA

Yes. You'll work for us.

PAUL

Learn all the trade. Not just the grotty part.

OUISA

Top to bottom.

PAUL

And live with you.

OUISA

No.

PAUL

Your kids are away.

OUISA

You should have your own place.

PAUL

You'll help me find a place?

OUISA

We'll help you find a place.

PAUL

I have no furniture.

OUISA

We'll help you out.

PAUL

I made a list of things I liked in the museum. Philadelphia Chippendale.

OUISA *(Bursts out laughing)*

Believe it or not, we have two Philadelphia Chippendale chairs—

PAUL

I'd rather have one nice piece than a room full of junk.

OUISA

Quality. Always. You'll have all that. Philadelphia
Chippendale.

PAUL

All I have to do is go to the police.

OUISA

Make it all history. Put it behind you.

PAUL

Tonight.

OUISA

It can't be tonight. I will take you tomorrow. We have
an auction tonight at Sotheby's—

PAUL

Bring me?

OUISA

I can't. It's black tie.

PAUL

I have black tie from a time I went to the Rainbow Room. Have you ever been to the Rainbow Room?

OUISA

Yes.

PAUL

What time do you have to be there?

OUISA

Eight o'clock.

PAUL

It's five-thirty now. You could come get me now and take me to the police tonight and then go to Sotheby's—

OUISA

We're going to drinks before at the Pierre.

PAUL

Japanese?

OUISA

Germans.

PAUL

You're just like my father.

OUISA

Which father?

PAUL

Sidney!

(Pause)

OUISA

Paul. He's not your father. And Flanders is not your father.

(FLAN *comes in, dressed.*)

FLAN

Oh fuck. We have drinks with the Japanese at six-fifteen—Get off that fucking phone. Is it that kid? Get him out of our life! Get off that phone or I'll rip it out of the wall!

(OUISA *looks at* FLAN.)

OUISA *(To* PAUL*)*

Paul, I made a mistake. It is not the Germans. We will come right now and get you. Where are you? Tell me? I'll take you to the police. They will treat you with dignity.

PAUL

I'm in the lobby of the Waverly movie theater on Sixth Avenue and Third Street.

OUISA

We'll be there in half an hour.

PAUL

I'll give you fifteen minutes grace time.

OUISA

We'll be there. Paul. We love you.

PAUL

Ouisa. I love you. Ouisa Kittredge. Hey? Bring a pink shirt.

OUISA

We'll have a wonderful life.

(She hangs up.
PAUL *goes into the dark.)*

OUISA

We can skip the shmoozing. Pick the boy up, take him to the police and be at Sotheby's before eight.

(THE DETECTIVE appears.)

FLAN

He's at the Waverly Theater. Sixth Avenue and Third Street. The lobby.

OUISA

We promised we would bring him to you. He's special. Remember that he's special. Honor our promise.

(THE DETECTIVE nods and goes.)

OUISA *(To us)*

We go. Traffic on the FDR.

FLAN *(To us)*

We get there. I run into the theater. No one.

OUISA

A young man. Black. Have you seen him?

FLAN (*To us*)

The girl in the box office said the police were there, had arrested a young man. Dragged him kicking, screaming into a squad car. He was a kid waiting for his family. We could never get through or find out.

OUISA (*To us*)

We weren't family.

FLAN (*To us*)

That detective was transferred.

OUISA (*To us*)

And we didn't know Paul's name.

We called the precinct.
Another precinct had made the arrest.
Why? Were there other charges?
We couldn't find out.

We weren't family.
We didn't know Paul's name.

We called the district attorney's office.
We weren't family.
We didn't know Paul's name.

I called the Criminal Courts.
I wasn't family.
I didn't know Paul's name.

FLAN

Why does it mean so much to you?

OUISA

He wanted to be us. Everything we are in the world,

this paltry thing—our life—he wanted it. He stabbed himself to get in here. He envied us. We're not enough to be envied.

FLAN

Like the papers said. We have hearts.

OUISA

Having a heart is not the point. We were hardly taken in. We believed him—for a few hours. He did more for us in a few hours than our children ever did. He wanted to be your child. Don't let that go. He sat out in that park and said that man is my father. He's in trouble and we don't know how to help him.

FLAN

Help him? He could've killed me. And you.

OUISA

You were attracted to him—

FLAN

Cut me out of that pathology! You are on your own—

OUISA

Attracted by youth and his talent and the embarrassing prospect of being in the movie version of *Cats*. Did you put that in your *Times* piece? And we turn him into an anecdote to dine out on. Or dine in on. But it was an experience. I will not turn him into an anecdote. How do we fit what happened to us into life without turning it into an anecdote with no teeth and a punch line you'll mouth over and over for years to come. "Tell the story about the imposter who came into our lives—" "That reminds me of the time this boy—." And we become these human juke boxes spilling out these anecdotes. But it was an experience. How do we *keep* the experience?

FLAN *(To us)*
That's why I love paintings. Cezanne. The problems he brought up are the problems painters are still dealing with. Color. Structure. Those are problems.

OUISA
There is color in my life, but I'm not aware of any structure.

FLAN *(To us)*
Cezanne would leave blank spaces in his canvasses if he couldn't account for the brush stroke, give a reason for the color.

OUISA
Then I am a collage of unaccounted-for brush strokes. I am all random. God, Flan, how much of your life can you account for?

FLAN
Are you drunk? The Cezanne sale went through. We are rich. Geoffrey's rich. Tonight there's a Matisse we'll get and next month there's a Bonnard and after that—

(She considers him.)

OUISA
These are the times I would take a knife and dig out your heart. Answer me? How much of your—

FLAN
—life can I account for! *All*! I am a gambler!

(*Pause*)

OUISA

We're a terrible match.

OUISA (*To us*)

Time passes.

OUISA

I read today that a young man committed suicide in Riker's Island. Tied a shirt around his neck and hanged himself. Was it the pink shirt? This burst of color? The pink shirt. Was it Paul? Who are you? We never found out who you are?

FLAN

I'm sure it's not him. He'll be back. We haven't heard the last of him. The imagination. He'll find a way.

FLAN (*To us*)

We have to go. An auction.

FLAN

I'll get the elevator.

(FLAN *goes.*)

OUISA (*To us*)

But if it was the pink shirt. Pink. A burst of pink. The Sistine Chapel. They've cleaned it and it's all these colors.

FLAN'S VOICE

Darling—

(OUISA *starts to go. She looks up.* PAUL *is there, wearing the pink shirt.*)

PAUL

The Kandinsky. It's painted on two sides.

(*He glows for a moment and is gone.*
She considers. She smiles.
The Kandinsky begins its slow revolve.)

T H E E N D

ABOUT THE AUTHOR

John Guare's *The House of Blue Leaves* won the New York Drama Critics Circle Award for Best American Play of 1971 and received four Tony awards in its revival at Lincoln Center in 1986. His screenplay for Louis Malle's *Atlantic City* won the New York, Los Angeles, and National Film Critics Circle awards, as well as an Oscar nomination. Mr. Guare, a longtime council member of the Dramatists Guild, was elected in 1989 to the American Academy and Institute of Arts and Letters. He lives in New York with his wife, Adele Chatfield-Taylor.